YOU CHOOSE
BOOKS

ALCATRAZ

A CHILLING INTERACTIVE ADVENTURE

by Matt Chandler

CAPSTONE PRESS
a capstone imprint

You Choose Books are published by Capstone Press,
1710 Roe Crest Drive, North Mankato, Minnesota 56003
www.capstonepub.com

Library of Congress Cataloging-in-Publication Data
Cataloging-in-publication information is on file with the Library of Congress.
ISBN 978-1-5157-2580-0 (library binding)
ISBN 978-1-5157-2584-8 (ebook PDF)

Editorial Credits
Anthony Wacholtz, editor; Heidi Thompson, designer; Wanda Winch, media researcher; Laura Manthe, production specialist

Photo Credits
Corbis/Bettmann, 20, 93; Getty Images: The LIFE Picture Collection/Nat Farbman, 59; National Parks Service: Golden Gate National Recreation Area Park Archives, 90, FBI Alcatraz Escape Photo Collection, 25, Darlyne Sheppard Alcatraz Photo Collection, 31, 35, Interpretive Negative Collection, 64, 87, Marc Fischetti Alcatraz Photo Collection, 70, Weinhold Family Alcatraz Photo Collection, 67; News Dog Media: Sheila Sillery-Walsh, 104; Ocean View Publishing, 16, 23, 80; San Francisco History Center, San Francisco Public Library, 52; Shutterstock: Albo, 42, Anton_Ivanov, 75, Daniel DeSlover, 102, f8grapher, cover (top), 12, happykanppy, old paper painting design, Krivosheev Vitaly, cover (middle), kropic1, 6, Lynn Indrizzo, 47, Maciej Biedowski, 44, Plateresca, grunge label design, run4it, grunge paper painting design, saki80, grunge frame design, Tomi Murphy, 4, Vacclav, 11, wawri, 40, Zacarias Pereira da Mata, cover (bottom); SuperStock: JTB Photo, 94, Robert Huberman, 100; Thinkstock, davelasker, 89, MorelSO, 28

Printed in Canada.
009633F16

Table of Contents

INTRODUCTION 5

TERROR ON THE ROCK 7

EPILOGUE: THE ROCK.............................101

TIMELINE 106

GLOSSARY...108

OTHER PATHS TO EXPLORE..........110

READ MORE...111

INTERNET SITES...............................111

INDEX 112

INTRODUCTION

YOU are on the famous island fortress, Alcatraz. Its walls hold many secrets, dating back to its days as a military fort and then a prison. As you explore its mysterious hallways and cells, you're about to find out why so many people have found "The Rock" such a fascinating—and terrifying—place. Will you overcome your fear and escape the island? Or will you remain trapped within its walls forever?

Alcatraz Island has been a military reservation, a prison, and a national park.

TERROR ON THE ROCK

"Don't worry, they won't even know we're gone," you whisper to your best friend Taryn as you lean out across the railing of the ferry. The idea of a class trip to Alcatraz, the famous prison in California, would be exciting enough for most kids your age. But you've always been adventurous, as your teacher Mrs. Woodford says. She's strict, and she's leading the trip, so you know if there is going to be any real excitement on Alcatraz Island, you'll have to escape her watchful eye.

"But Mrs. Woodford says anyone who breaks the rules will be in detention until June!" Taryn says stubbornly.

Turn the page.

Taryn is the smartest student in your class, maybe the entire school. She spent two weeks reading everything she could about Alcatraz, and you'll need her help to find your way around.

"Come on, don't you want to see any of the really top-secret, behind-the-scenes stuff? I promise, we'll be back with the class before they even miss us," you say, giving Taryn a sly grin.

The ferry whistle pierces the early morning fog that hangs low over San Francisco Bay. You and Taryn look up, and in the distance is Alcatraz Federal Penitentiary. The main prison building, guard tower, and lighthouse catch your eye as you near the island.

As the boat docks, Mrs. Woodford gathers the students at the front and begins barking orders. You grab Taryn's hand and pull her toward the rear of the ferry.

"We can sneak away while Mrs. Woodford's explaining all of her rules," you tell Taryn. She pauses for a second then nods excitedly.

You tiptoe down the metal walkway. When you reach the bottom, you realize you haven't actually made a plan.

"We could climb along those huge boulders that line the island," you say. Taryn tenses up and digs her feet into the ground at your suggestion.

"No way. It looks dangerous," she says. "Let's start with the warden's house. Everyone else will be in the main building, and I've read some cool and creepy things about that place."

To climb the rocks along the water, turn to page 10.

To head for the warden's house, turn to page 44.

"It makes more sense to stay away from the buildings until the rest of the class is inside," you say to Taryn. She looks at you with reluctance but follows as you run toward the rocky edge of the island. As you near the shore, the ground becomes increasingly muddy. With each step your feet sink in deeper, like quicksand.

With some effort you reach the rocks and find a large boulder with a big flat surface. You carefully pull yourself up and face the prison, watching your classmates file inside single file like prisoners under Warden Woodford. Out of the corner of your eye, you see movement. You look toward the water and see a man paddling on a dirty yellow raft.

"Taryn," you say softly but urgently. "Look!"

"What? I don't see anything but the water," she says.

Alcatraz is often named the United States' top tourist destination. It is also one of America's most haunted places.

"I swear I saw a man in some sort of homemade raft …"

She cuts you off. "Why would someone be in a raft way out here?" Before you can answer, her voice lowers and she whispers another question. "What color was it?"

Turn the page.

The lighthouse is the tallest structure on Alcatraz Island.

"It was hard to see in the choppy water, and I only saw it for a second, but I'm sure it was yellow," you tell her.

Taryn gives you an uneasy look. "Yellow like the raincoats," she mutters. When you give her a questioning look, she explains. "I read about three prisoners in 1962 who made homemade rafts out of raincoats. They escaped, never to be seen again. The raincoats were yellow." A chill runs down your spine.

"I'm going to check out the lighthouse," Taryn says. "You can do what you want, but I'm not going any closer to that water."

To follow Taryn up the hill toward the lighthouse, turn to page 14.

To look for the man on the raft, turn to page 17.

"Okay, wait up," you yell to Taryn, who has started to trudge toward the lighthouse. You approach the imposing cylinder and reach for the rusted door handle. It creaks as it opens, and you feel a rush of frigid air even though it's a warm day. You ignore it and race up the metal stairs, eager to see the view from the top.

When you're halfway up, you hear a noise—a dull banging from down below you.

"What was that?" Taryn squeals, panic in her voice.

"Probably just a squirrel or something," you say, trying to reassure yourself as much as your friend. "Let's go! We're almost at the top."

At last you step onto the main observation deck and take in the amazing view. You can see across the bay, all the way to San Francisco.

"I'm going back inside," Taryn calls out, and you hear the door clang shut as she disappears.

As soon as she leaves, you hear the banging again, this time louder than before. You peer out toward the water, and you see the raft again! It's unmistakable from your new vantage point. The man is there too, dressed in what looks like an old-fashioned prisoner's outfit. He raises what looks like a homemade oar from the water and shakes it in your direction. Your hands are clammy, and your body begins to shake. Something's not right.

Then, in the blink of an eye, the man from the raft is up on land near the entrance to the lighthouse. How did that happen? You never took your eyes off him, but somehow he traveled hundreds of feet in a split second!

"HELP! HE'S GOT ME! HELP ME!"

Turn the page.

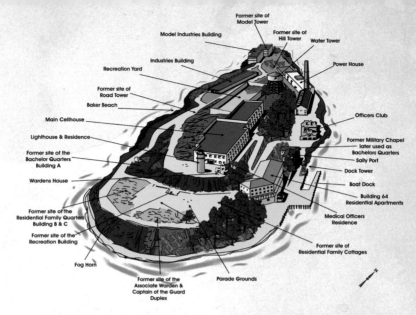

Both civilians and prisoners alike have called Alcatraz Island home.

Your thoughts are broken by Taryn's screams. You run to the door and yank it open. Down the short hall stands a figure in the doorway, his back to you. He has what looks like the barrel of a gun over one shoulder. His other hand is wrapped around Taryn. You freeze, unsure what to do next.

To try to save Taryn yourself, turn to page 19.

To run for help, turn to page 22.

There is no way you are missing the chance to find the man in the raft. You yell to Taryn that you'll catch up with her.

Ahead there is a wiry, overgrown bush jutting out of the rocky terrain. Once you get past that, you should have a clear view of where you saw the man in the raft paddle away. Balancing on a large rock, you stretch and try to step to the next one.

Suddenly, you lose your balance and fall to the ground, landing in a shallow pool of water. As you steady yourself on your hands and knees, you see a face staring back at you from the pool, but it isn't your reflection. It looks like an old man with a graying beard and crooked teeth. You jump to your feet, and the face disappears. Was it your imagination?

Turn the page.

Your thoughts are interrupted by the sound of two voices up ahead. The choppy water is crashing against the rocks, making it hard to hear. You pick up bits and pieces of the conversation.

"I'll finish ... have the gun ... just use a rock."

Use a rock? Gun? Who are these men? Park rangers? Yeah, that's it, you think. Probably just security guards making their rounds. But what if you're wrong?

To turn away from the voices, turn to page 34.

To follow the voices, turn to page 37.

Taryn is your best friend, and there is no way you're leaving her. You creep down the hall, your body shaking. You pick up an old pipe propped against the wall. You hope it will be enough to knock the man down and allow you and Taryn to escape.

You edge closer and can hear Taryn's whimpers. You raise the pipe, but suddenly the door at the bottom of the lighthouse opens with a bang. The man holding Taryn turns, and you come face to face with Machine Gun Kelly, the infamous gangster! Though he isn't a big man, Kelly's appearance is terrifying. His skin is pale and transparent, and his eyes are lifeless. Kelly was transferred off Alcatraz decades ago, but apparently his ghost has returned!

Turn the page.

George "Machine Gun" Kelly was accused of crimes varying from robbery to kidnapping to smuggling. He became a prisoner at Alcatraz in September 1934.

Your eyes meet Taryn's. You know it's your fault for convincing her to sneak away from the class. You consider trying to swing your pipe through the transparent man, but you don't get the chance.

Soundlessly, instantly, the man from the raft has reached the top of the stairs. Taryn's eyes widen as the man raises his rotting, wooden oar over your head. You turn just in time to see it coming down on you. Your final thought before it all goes black is, *I'm so sorry, Taryn.*

THE END

To follow another path, turn to page 13.
To learn more about Alcatraz, turn to page 101.

You don't want to leave Taryn, but you can't help her escape by yourself. You know you're no match for that guy. You turn and run for the stairs, leaping down four at a time until you reach the bottom.

You run to the heavy iron exit door and pull, but it won't budge. It's the same door you came through five minutes earlier—how could it be stuck now? You look around for another door, but all you see are small windows.

You stumble around the room looking for a tool to pry the door open. Suddenly you trip and hit the ground hard. You pick yourself up and look back to see what you fell over.

In the floor you see what looks like a trap door. You reach for the handle and pull, and the old wooden door gives an eerie creak as it lifts up.

Dungeon cells were located deep in the cellblock basement.

You can see a crude set of stairs built into the ground going down to a tunnel. You've read about the secret tunnels of Alcatraz, but you figured they were just an urban legend. You're terrified at the thought of going into the dark, musty tunnel below the earth, but how else will you get out of the lighthouse and get help for Taryn?

To try to pry open the exit door, turn to page 24.

To follow the tunnel underground, turn to page 28.

You can't force yourself to go down into the darkness of the underground tunnel. You've got to find a way to get the lighthouse door open and escape! You look around and see an old pickax leaning against the wall. You grab it and drag it toward the door. Maybe you can wedge it in the crack and pry open the metal door.

You try to force the sharp edge of the ax into the doorframe, but the door doesn't budge. Frustrated, you bang it against the door. Sparks fly. But the ax is heavy, and soon you collapse to the floor. You're starting to think you're never going to make it out of the lighthouse.

When you think of Taryn still trapped by that horrible man, you pull yourself to your feet and begin wildly swinging the ax at the door again. The head of the ax crashes down onto the door handle and shatters it. You're shocked as the door swings open and sunlight pours in.

You run out and head straight for the main prison to find help, but the sound of glass shattering stops you in your tracks. You turn back to see hunks of glass raining down from the top of the lighthouse.

"HELP! HELP ME!" Taryn screams.

Frank Morris and John and Clarence Anglin spent three months digging through air vents with sharpened spoons before their escape on June 11, 1962. No one knows if they made it to freedom or died trying.

Turn the page.

You realize there's no time to get help. You don't care if you're no match for Taryn's captor—you have to help her!

You start to run back toward the lighthouse, but you see a shadowy figure behind Taryn in the window. It looks like the same man, but you can see right through his body. You're terrified, but you know you've still got to try to save Taryn.

You rush inside the lighthouse and run into the man from the raft. As you rush past him, your arm passes right through his body! He's no man. He's the spirit of a dead prisoner who tried to escape Alcatraz in 1962!

You're so shocked staring into the face of a dead man, you forget all about Taryn. In a voice that sounds hollow and unlike any you've ever heard, the spirit whispers to you.

"Sorry kid, but nobody ever escapes The Rock. Nobody." In the blink of an eye, the ghost of the prisoner is upon you. Your body stiffens, unable to move as the dead man makes you his latest victim.

THE END

To follow another path, turn to page 13.
To learn more about Alcatraz, turn to page 101.

The area below Cellblock A is known as the Spanish Dungeon. Rumor has it that the prison's worst inmates were sent there for punishment.

With the door stuck, you figure the tunnel is your best chance to get help for Taryn. It's got to lead to a building with more people. You hold your breath and creep down the concrete steps into the darkness.

Using the light coming through the cracks in the ceiling, you inch your way down the tunnel. Before long, the silence is disrupted by a faint noise up ahead. It sounds like something scraping against the rocks. You stop and listen. The scratching is getting louder. Then you hear the voice.

"Go back where you came from!"

The raspy whisper sends a chill over you. A stone from the wall flies past you, crashing into the other side of the tunnel. You drop to the ground and cover your head.

"THIS IS YOUR LAST WARNING— GET OUT!"

Two, three, four more stones fly from the wall, each whizzing past your head and slamming into the opposite wall before smashing to the ground.

Turn the page.

From a hole in the wall to your left, you see an arm reach out toward you. It looks human with a tattered sleeve hanging off of it, but the hand is bony and covered in gray skin with long, filthy nails. You instantly think of the zombies you've seen on TV.

Without even standing up, you scramble past the hole. Then you jump up and sprint through the darkness. You hear the voice of the dead over your shoulder.

"RUN, RUN! AND DON'T EVER COME BACK!"

You see a door ahead and speed up, hitting it hard with your body. It flies open and you stumble into a huge industrial kitchen. You run past stoves and sinks that haven't been used in decades.

Metal bars separated the kitchen area from the dining hall.

"HELP! HELP ME!" you scream, hoping someone will hear you. As you push through the double doors of the kitchen, you run headfirst into something as solid as a brick wall. You look up and into the cold blue eyes of a man dressed in ragged prison denim.

Turn the page.

"This ain't your lucky day kid," the prisoner says. He picks you up with one hand. You kick and thrash as he drags you toward the main cellblock.

"What do you want with me?" you manage to stammer between sobs. "Let me go, please."

The man doesn't speak. He just grunts and drags you to the last cell at the end of the hall. With a shove, he tosses you into the cell and you crash into Taryn. You can't believe you found her!

"Are you okay?" you ask your friend. "Are you hurt?"

"I'm scared," she says, trembling.

"Ain't nothing to be scared of," the weathered old convict growls. "It'll all be over for you soon enough."

He slams the door and you hear a key turn. How are you going to escape? Before you have time to even think of a plan, the man is back with a pack of other prisoners. They are all dressed in Alcatraz denim with their prison numbers on their shirts, but it's the only thing that makes them appear human. Their eyes are hollow black orbs. Their skin is sickly gray and transparent, yet at the same time it gives off a ghostly glow.

You watch in terror as the prisoners pass through the bars of the cell as though they aren't there. They close in on you and Taryn, looking eager to have you join them for an eternity in Alcatraz.

THE END

To follow another path, turn to page 13.
To learn more about Alcatraz, turn to page 101.

Between the face in the water, the strange man on the raft, and the disturbing conversation you overheard, you've had enough. You turn and start climbing up the hill toward the prison.

"Hey kid, you aren't supposed to be down here. Don't move!" You glance back and see the man from the raft. He is coming toward you, but unlike your struggles with the rocks, he seems to pass through them as though they aren't there. Fear kicks in. You take off, leaping from rock to rock, trying to escape the raft man.

"I said don't move! I'm coming to get you!" he yells, his voice getting closer with each word.

You take one final jump, and your sneakers land on the flat ground of the island. Just when you think you're free, you feel a hand grab your shoulder. The grip is so tight you can't move.

Guards were present at all times to watch over prisoners.

You turn back and see the raft man has disappeared—there is no one near you! And yet, you can still feel the hand on your shoulder. You try to run as you feel the invisible fingers tighten around you. What's happening to you? What's got you?

Turn the page.

35

"HELP! HELP ME!" you scream as loud as you can. You're still a ways off from the closest building, and you doubt anyone can hear you.

With your free arm you swing your elbow wildly behind you. Surprisingly, the grip on your shoulder releases, and you take off running. The minute it takes you to reach the entrance to Alcatraz feels like the longest minute of your life. As you burst through the door into the crowd of tourists, you've never been so happy to be in the nice, boring safety of a group. You suspect that no one will ever believe your chilling brush with the ghosts of Alcatraz.

THE END

To follow another path, turn to page 13.
To learn more about Alcatraz, turn to page 101.

You know it's crazy, but you have to follow the voices. Curiosity always wins. Your heart is beating and your palms are sweaty, but still you inch forward along the rocks. You hear the men again, this time their voices louder.

"Enough with these tourists treatin' this place like a hotel," one man says.

"Yeah, I hope we get our hands on a few of 'em. They'll wish they never set foot on Alcatraz Island," the other man snarls.

You peek around the corner and see two shadowy figures. Instead of walking along the rocks, they seem to float effortlessly through them. Both men are surrounded by a white light, a hazy orb that follows them as they move toward you. As the tall one raises an arm, you see he is missing all of his fingers.

Turn the page.

Ghosts! Are they dead prisoners? Former guards? You don't know, and you're not going to wait to find out. You've got a split second to decide what to do.

To jump into the water to find the raft, go to page 39.

To hide behind the biggest rock, turn to page 41.

You look to your left and see the choppy waters of San Francisco Bay. You figure if you jump in, you might be able to find the raft you saw earlier. You take a big breath, hold your nose, and jump.

You hit the icy cold water hard. As your head bobs up, you feel the current pulling you away from the island—fast. It was a mistake to jump, but it's too late now. You know your only chance to survive is for someone on shore to rescue you.

"HEEEELLLLPPPP!!!" you scream, before taking in a big mouthful of water. It's more than a mile across the bay to San Francisco, and you're already freezing. Your arms feel like they are on fire, and your body is going numb from the cold. You paddle faster and faster, but the harder you work, the farther the current drags you away.

Turn the page.

The distance across San Francisco Bay is about 1.5 miles (2.4 kilometers).

You look around hoping there might be a fishing boat nearby. Instead, you see what you instantly recognize as a dorsal fin. San Francisco Bay is known for its sharks. You see a second fin, then a third. You're too weak to swim, scream, or even be scared anymore. As the sharks draw near, you close your eyes and slip under the surface.

THE END

To follow another path, turn to page 13.
To learn more about Alcatraz, turn to page 101.

You crouch down as low as possible, hoping the ghosts will pass you by. You hear the voices again. As they pass by the rock you're hiding behind, your foot slips, and some loose stones fall. The dead men turn back toward you. You're trapped.

In a panic you grab a rock and throw it at them. The stone passes right through the taller of the two men, and he laughs. "Nice try kid, but you can't hurt us—we're already dead!"

You turn and start running over the rocky hill toward the prison. But before you've taken two steps, the two specters instantly appear in front of you.

"You can't outrun us either kid. Why don't you stop and make this easy on yourself?"

Turn the page.

Frank Lee Morris and the Anglin brothers created dummy heads to fool guards while they escaped.

With a deep breath, you charge straight at the dead convicts. You close your eyes and barrel toward the biggest man. Just like the stone, you pass through him! You never break stride, reaching the top of the hill in no time. Looking back, the ghosts are gone. They must not want to return to the prison they once escaped.

As you run toward the prison to find your class and Taryn, you realize how lucky you are. You dared to explore the shores of Alcatraz Island, where more than a dozen men were shot or drowned trying to escape. Unlike those unfortunate souls, you'll leave the island alive.

THE END

To follow another path, turn to page 13.
To learn more about Alcatraz, turn to page 101.

"Wait up, I'm coming!" you call out to Taryn. You jog up the rugged terrain toward the prison. The warden's house stands to the side of the main prison building. You can't wait to see it. You imagine it to be a grand mansion. As you trudge up over the crest of the hill, though, you see something quite different.

Alcatraz was the first U.S. fort built on the west coast.

"What happened to it?" Taryn asks, looking in amazement at the burned out shell of a building. All that's left of the once magnificent home are four cement walls. The windows, doors, and virtually everything else is gone. The ruins of the home are surrounded by a low railing.

"Maybe we should skip this and go check out the prison," Taryn says. "That's what we came here for anyway."

To explore the warden's house, turn to page 46.

To head to the main prison, turn to page 77.

"Come on, it's just an old building—at least what's left of one," you tell Taryn as you climb over the railing.

You head toward where you imagine the front door once was. As you move into what remains of a large room, a freezing chill comes over you. The sun has come out from behind the clouds, but in this moment, you feel trapped in a blizzard.

Then you hear a noise overhead. You look up to find a large cinderblock falling right at you! You sidestep quickly, and the cinderblock crashes to the ground.

"See, this place is dangerous! We shouldn't be here," Taryn says. You decide she's right, figuring it's best to get out before any more loose rocks fall. You turn back toward where you came in just as another large piece of concrete falls from above. You jump to the side and it crashes right next to you!

The warden's house was used until 1963. In 1970 a fire engulfed the building. Today it stands in ruin.

You cover your head and run for the door. But you smash into what feels like a brick wall and fall back to the ground. You look up and there's nothing in front of you. How can that be?

You pull yourself up and try to walk through the door, but again you hit an invisible wall. Something is keeping you from leaving, but what?

To try to escape through the back, turn to page 48.

To climb out one of the window holes, turn to page 50.

Let's go!" you yell as you grab Taryn's arm. You run to the center of the house, through the flying debris. With jagged rocks and pieces of cement whizzing past your heads, you and Taryn race for the back of the building.

You emerge from the room, somehow having avoided serious injury. You're eager to leave the house, but there's a man standing in the back doorway. His clothes look old-fashioned, with a top hat and a long coat with tails. He has long, wide sideburns and a cold, dead stare. He doesn't look like he's here to rescue you!

"Didn't you read the sign?" the man asks. Before you can reply, he raises both arms toward the ceiling and begins to violently shake. His eyes roll back in his head, and you and Taryn drop to your knees in fear. As he motions, chunks of the ceiling begin to fall again, much heavier this time.

"YOU WERE WARNED!" the man yells, his breath leaving a cloud of steam in the air. You curl up on the ground as rocks begin striking you. As the old warden's home begins to collapse around you, you see the man mysteriously float up into the sky, an evil laugh coming from deep inside him. As the largest wall of the warden's home comes crashing down, your world goes dark.

THE END

To follow another path, turn to page 13.
To learn more about Alcatraz, turn to page 101.

"Follow me!" you yell to Taryn as you scramble away from the flying rocks, toward the large window up ahead. You're almost there when you feel something pull at your feet. You look down and see that you're standing on a large white section of the floor that seems to be moving. The patch of floor begins to bubble up, and you feel your shoes sinking in like it's quicksand! You pull as hard as you can but your feet won't budge. You look back at Taryn, who is also struggling to pull her feet free.

"Grab my hand!" a voice barks. You swivel around and see a tall man with a bony face and long, stringy hair. He is reaching through the wall where the window once was. His skin is a sickly gray, and he looks like the last person you'd want to touch. But your feet are stuck in the cement. What choice do you have?

Then you have an idea. You could untie your shoes and try to jump out of them onto the hard floor.

"Give me your hand before you die!" the man cries, his booming voice echoing through the empty shell of a building.

To try to jump out of your shoes, turn to page 52.

To take the man's hand, turn to page 54.

There's no way you trust this creepy stranger who appeared out of nowhere and wants you to take his hand. The cement is covering your sneakers, but if you can untie the laces, you might be able to wiggle free.

James A. Johnston was a warden at Alcatraz from 1934–1938.

"Loosen your shoes," you tell Taryn, reaching down to your own feet. "We're going to jump!"

"TAKE MY HAND NOW!" the man's voice booms, sending a shiver through you. You look back at him just as more rocks begin flying through the air. One is coming straight at the man, but instead of hitting him, it passes right through his body and lands outside.

"Let's go!" you yell. With all the strength you can muster, you leap up, reaching for the dark, solid concrete to your right. You land with a hard thud and stumble to your feet. The dead man growls at you as you begin to run, "Get back here, trespassers!"

To run toward the main prison, turn to page 56.

To run for the boat dock, turn to page 57.

53

Your whole body is shaking as you reach for the man. As soon as your fingers touch, a bolt of electricity courses through your body. You turn back to Taryn and see her shaking from the shock, a panicked look in her eyes. The pain is like nothing you've ever experienced. The cement holding you in place suddenly begins to crumble around you, freeing your feet. You reach back for Taryn and pull her forward as her feet release from the ground too.

You're now face to face with the scariest looking man you've ever seen. His clothes are filthy and tattered. His rotten teeth and lifeless eyes fill a sunken face. He definitely doesn't work here, you think to yourself.

"We got separated from our class," you stammer, hoping he will let you go.

"No you didn't!" he barked at you, his face twisting into a scowl. "Don't lie to me. You snuck away to cause trouble. But don't worry. I'm going to send you back!"

"We tried to leave, but we couldn't get through the front door," you say, your voice beginning to crack.

"Well then, let me help you," the man hisses. He waves one of his skeleton-like arms at you, and both you and Taryn are instantly hurled backward off your feet. Your bodies crash to the ground outside.

The look on the ghost's face turns from anger to sadness. "I'm stuck here for eternity," he says. "There's no reason you have to be stuck here too." He turns his back to you as his body slowly fades away.

THE END

To follow another path, turn to page 13.
To learn more about Alcatraz, turn to page 101.

Running through the shell of the warden's house isn't easy. You dodge flying rocks as you try to find a way out. You run for the side of the building with the ghost of the dead man following close behind.

Up ahead you see a huge hole in the crumbling wall. Without breaking stride, you run straight through it, relieved to be outside again.

"That way, let's go!" you yell, pointing to the main prison building. Your legs are burning and you're drenched in sweat, but your adrenaline pushes you on toward the building.

As you and Taryn reach the building, you come across two doors. One is the main visitor entrance. The other is marked with a sign that reads, "Security Office."

To go through the security door, turn to page 65.

To run through the main door, turn to page 66.

You've had enough of this place. Your best chance to escape Alcatraz alive is to get back to the boat. You grab Taryn's hand and run for the open window. You can see San Francisco Bay in the opening. You just need to make it out the window and to the bottom of the hill.

"JUMP!" you yell to Taryn. You both leap in the air, hurling yourselves toward the opening. Chunks of cement are flying around, and you know the dead man is right behind you.

You hit the ground hard and roll forward, then spring to your feet. You look around and realize nothing is as it was. The boats that were just at the docks are gone. The signs welcoming tourists to Alcatraz aren't there. Everything looks different. But how?

Turn the page.

You turn back toward the ruins of the warden's house and see a beautiful three-story mansion! The front door opens and two men come out, deep in conversation as they walk toward the prison. You shake your head and blink. Somehow, when you jumped through the window, you landed back in time when Alcatraz Island was a working prison!

Up ahead you see a group of rough-looking prisoners, followed by two guards with machine guns. Where are the boats? How do you get back? Your mind is racing. You've got to move before someone sees you!

To climb back through the window, turn to page 60.

To run for help, turn to page 62.

WARNING
PERSONS PROCURING OR CONCEALING ESCAPE OF PRISONERS ARE SUBJECT TO PROSECUTION AND IMPRISONMENT

Thirty-six prisoners tried to escape from the island. Only two were successful. Seven were shot and killed, and two drowned. Another five were never found.

"We must have gone through some kind of time portal," you tell Taryn, not believing your own words. "Maybe if we climb back through the window, we'll return to modern time!"

You scamper back and peer through the window. Unlike the empty hole you jumped out, you are now staring through a large glass window covered in curtains. You can't see inside, but you realize you don't have any choice. You reach for the window and slide it up. You hear soft music coming from inside and smell delicious food.

"Wait here," you tell Taryn, figuring you'd better check it out first. Pulling yourself up, you land on the floor. Gone is the rough concrete, replaced with thick, soft carpet. The home is beautiful, and the room you're in has a roaring fire blazing in the corner. You hear voices in the other room and decide to follow the sounds and smells.

Then you see a man standing in the corner, watching you. You think about running, but in your heart you know it's too late. In the time it takes you to blink, he is at your side.

"You didn't really think you were gonna escape did you, kid?" With a wave of his hand, the dead man extinguishes the fire, and the room goes dark. You can feel his hot breath on your face as he leans in to whisper what will be the last words you ever hear: "You should have stayed with your class."

THE END

To follow another path, turn to page 13.
To learn more about Alcatraz, turn to page 101.

None of this makes any sense, but your instincts tell you to run. Together you and Taryn begin to sprint toward the main prison building. Your heart is racing and you don't know what's happening, but you know you need to find an adult. Your thoughts are interrupted by the voice of the dead man coming from behind you.

"You can't escape!" he bellows. "You're mine!" You run faster, trying to figure out how the dead man came back in time with you and what he wants. You can see the main entrance of the prison ahead. You're almost there! Unfortunately, you're no match for a ghost. In a flash, the dead man is standing in front of you.

You turn to Taryn and see she has closed her eyes. You both fall to the ground, scared and exhausted as the ghost is upon you, his lifeless body now floating above the ground.

"Stop your shaking and whimpering," the dead man snarls. "I ain't gonna kill you. That'd be too easy."

The ghost raises a bony hand toward you and Taryn, and at the same time, your body rises into the air. You kick your legs, but it's no use. With a wave of his hand, the ghost sends you and Taryn hurtling toward the stone wall of the prison. You brace for the impact, but your bodies pass effortlessly through the wall. The two of you collapse onto cold, hard cement. Stumbling to your feet, you realize you're inside a locked cell.

"Nice to see I've finally got some company," a man hisses.

Al Capone steps forward out of the shadows. Taryn gasps and clings to your arm, but you are frozen in place.

Turn the page.

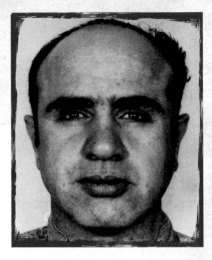

Al Capone was a notorious mobster in Chicago. He was sentenced to trial in 1931 and sent to Alcatraz two years later after he was caught bribing guards.

"Let me share some stories of when I was a gangster boss," Capone says with a smile. "Those were some good times."

When you left your house this morning you had no idea you would end up a prisoner locked away in Alcatraz. No one knows you're here. You and Taryn will be trapped on this island of despair forever with your new ghostly roommate.

THE END

To follow another path, turn to page 13.
To learn more about Alcatraz, turn to page 101.

Finding a security guard sounds like the safest choice. You open the door and pull Taryn inside.

"We'll be safe in here," you say, twisting the big bolt that locks the door.

"He's a ghost!" she screams in your face. "He can float right through that door, that wall, and probably right through us!"

She's right. You can't outrun the dead. You need another plan. You look around for another escape route when you see the door begin to glow.

The glowing door illuminates the room, and you see the dead man pass through it. The floor begins to shake beneath your feet, and you fall to the ground. You close your eyes tight, not wanting to see the end.

THE END

To follow another path, turn to page 13.
To learn more about Alcatraz, turn to page 101.

"We should go in the main entrance," Taryn insists. "That's where everyone else will be. Safety in numbers, right?"

She doesn't wait for an answer. She runs up the ramp to the main door, and you follow closely behind. Inside the door a man in uniform greets you. He's tall, skinny, and the name over his shirt pocket says, "Stites."

"Hey there, you two look like you've seen a ghost," the man chuckles.

"We got lost … need to find our class … being chased … help us!" Your words come out jumbled up as you try to catch your breath.

"Slow down, you're OK," he replies. "I can help you find your group." A wide grin spreads across his face.

"You said you were being chased," Stites says as he leads you and Taryn down the long corridor of cellblock B. "It wasn't that old fool from the warden's house was it?"

"H-h-how do you know about him?" you stammer, stopping in your tracks and staring up at the guard.

Guards and their families lived on the island. At any time, around 300 civilians called Alcatraz home.

Turn the page.

"Don't worry," he says, placing an icy hand on your shoulder. "This place is crawling with the dead souls of some of the worst men who ever walked this earth, but I'm one of the good ones. Stick with me and I'll get you two out of here alive."

The freezing touch of his hand send chills down your spine. Then it hits you: Stites is a ghost! Can you really trust him?

To follow Stites into the cellblock, go to page 69.

To run away, turn to page 73.

It may be crazy, but following a friendly ghost seems like the best choice you have. With the ghostly guard leading the way, you walk down the cellblock, passing the cells of some of the most dangerous prisoners of Alcatraz.

"Stay close to me, kids," Stites says, as you and Taryn jog to catch up. "We're about to pass Capone's cell and Al ain't been in too good a mood lately."

Up ahead you hear the soft sound of a banjo coming from a cell. As you pass by, you see a balding stocky man picking away at the instrument. When he sees you, he scowls and sets the banjo down.

"Don't even think about it, Capone," Stites says, but it's too late. Capone stands and in an instant passes through the bars of his cell. He steps up to Stites, their faces inches apart.

Turn the page.

The prison had hardened steel bars, a mechanical locking system, and metal detectors.

"Whaddya doin' bringin' KIDS down MY cellblock?" Capone yells.

"Back in your cell, Capone, before I use that precious banjo of yours for firewood!" replies Stites. Then he turns to you. "Keep moving kids. I'll take care of Al."

With Stites keeping Capone at bay, you and Taryn walk as fast as you can down the corridor. You can hear the ghosts arguing behind you, but you're too scared to look back.

"Let's head for that door," you say, pointing to an exit sign up ahead. A streak of light flashes past, and then Stites is in front of you.

He says, "Listen kids, this is as far as I can take you. I'm a prison ghost, and I can't survive outside these walls."

You shudder, wondering if you'll run into the ghost from the warden's house. Stites seems to anticipate your thought.

"Don't worry about that guy," he reassures you. "He's just an old party guest of the warden's who likes to hang around and scare people. He's just having fun. Being dead gets boring."

Turn the page.

"Now Al," he continues, "he would kill you both if he could catch you, but he can't leave the building either. His soul is trapped inside these walls forever, so git while you can!"

Stites pushes open the door, and you smile as the sun hits you. Capone can't leave Alcatraz, you tell yourself. You're going to be OK.

You and Taryn run down the steep hill toward the boats. As you near the docks, you see the familiar faces of your classmates and Mrs. Woodford. You've never been so happy to see your teacher in your life!

"We made it!" you yell as you run faster toward the group. You feel so lucky to be alive. You came face-to-face with the ghosts of Alcatraz and lived to tell about it!

THE END

To follow another path, turn to page 13.
To learn more about Alcatraz, turn to page 101.

There's no way you're following a ghost anywhere, no matter how friendly he seems. You motion to Taryn to run, and the two of you take off.

"Aw, kids, that's a bad decision!" Stites yells.

You realize it's almost time to go. You need to make it back to the docks. But with Stites between you and the main gate, you have to find another way out of Alcatraz.

Up ahead you see a red sign lit up with the word "Exit." You and Taryn push the door open and find yourself in a courtyard outside the prison. The wind has picked up, and you shiver from the bone-chilling cold. But right now all you care about is making it to the boat. You begin to run, your heart racing as your eyes dart wildly, looking for any sign of Stites or the dead man from the warden's house.

Turn the page.

You scamper down the hill, weaving around the jagged rocks that dot the side of Alcatraz Island. Up ahead, you can see the boat you arrived on with a group of passengers nearby. You're so excited to make it back that you don't see the boulder in your path.

"Oooowwww!" you wail, as you tumble head over heels. You bounce up just in time to look back and see the ominous outline of a man at the top of the hill. You see him raise a gun. Did he see you?

You don't wait to find out. Bloodied and bruised, you summon all your strength to keep moving, with Taryn close behind. You sigh with relief when you see Mrs. Woodford and the rest of your class. There is also a group of security men surrounding them.

The only way on and off the island is by ferry.

When you reach the boat, you collapse, exhausted. Mrs. Woodford runs up to you and Taryn.

"Are you two okay?" she asks. "We were worried sick about you!"

Turn the page.

"We are now," you whisper, closing your eyes and relaxing for the first time since your nightmare began. "I just want to go home."

Crossing the bay in the ferry, you turn back for one last look at Alcatraz. On top of the hill, you see the dead man from the warden's house. With his weapon over his shoulder, he is staring intently at the next ferry packed with tourists making its way to Alcatraz.

THE END

To follow another path, turn to page 13.
To learn more about Alcatraz, turn to page 101.

"You're right," you say. "We came here to see the prison."

You and Taryn head toward the main building. As you approach the entrance, you're surprised by how big the building is. This place doesn't look so scary. It's basically a museum.

You sneak in past the old man working the front desk and scurry down the hall, unsure of what lies ahead.

"Let's find The Birdman's cell," Taryn says, excited.

You reach into your back pocket and pull out an Alcatraz fact book you brought along for this very reason. You flip to the biography of The Birdman. His cell was No. 42 in D-Block of Alcatraz, the block where the worst prisoners were kept.

Turn the page.

"Are you sure you want to go down there?" you ask Taryn, trying to convince her with your tone to turn back. "I think The Hole is near his cell." The Hole was the place where prisoners were sent as a form of isolation. The stories of prisoners being beaten, starved, and going insane in The Hole were legendary in Alcatraz.

"We don't have to, if you're scared," she challenges you.

"I'm not scared. Let's go!" you reply confidently.

You follow the signs until you reach cellblock D. Then you follow the numbers until you reach D-42, longtime home of The Birdman.

The plaque outside of the cell tells you his real name was Robert Stroud. It also tells you two things that send a shiver down your spine:

Robert Stroud was sentenced to 12 years in prison for murder. While serving his time, Stroud killed a guard and was sentenced to death.

"So much for being a friendly old guy who took care of birds," you say to Taryn, your voice barely a whisper. You suddenly want to get as far away from cellblock D as possible. "Let's get out of here. This is boring," you lie.

To stay and explore cellblock D, turn to page 80.

To look for your class, turn to page 83.

Cellblock D had 36 cells known as confinement chambers, and 6 cells for solitary confinement.

"Come on, this is cool," Taryn says. "Let's at least check out The Hole. Then we can go outside."

You think she's crazy, but you agree to stay. Mostly you're just glad to get away from The Birdman's cell.

Walking along cellblock D, you notice a set of wet footprints on the cement. This is one of the most popular parts of the tour, yet there is only a single set of footprints.

You reach down and press your finger to the footprint. You pull back quickly, a thick, clear goo dripping from your hand.

"What do you think this is?" you ask. As you examine the gooey footprints, more footprints suddenly appear. You have a hard time believing it, but it looks like an invisible person is walking down the cellblock! The word *ectoplasm* flashes in your brain before Taryn screams.

You both begin to run, but in your panic, you miss the door leading outside. Instead, you turn and run straight into the last cell in The Hole. It is freezing cold there with frost built up on the bars and small window. You can see your breath.

Turn the page.

"What's happening?" Taryn stammers, her voice cracking from terror. Before you can answer, you hear a bang. The cell across from you has closed. BANG! BANG! BANG! The next three cell doors mysteriously slam shut.

You grab Taryn's arm and dive out of the cell. Your feet clear the door just as the cell slams shut.

"What happened?" Taryn asks, tears running down her face.

"I don't know, but we've got to get out of here, NOW!"

To run for the nearest exit, turn to page 92.

To go back to the main entrance to find help, turn to page 96.

You'd never let Taryn know it, but you just want to get out of here as fast as possible. Walking much faster than before, you race out of the cellblock and back toward the main gate of Alcatraz.

As you walk, your sneakers squeak against the cement floors of the prison. Taryn's footsteps produce light thuds alongside you. But then you hear a third set of steps making a clicking noise on the floor. Hoping that you've found a museum worker, you turn to ask for help. But the long narrow hallway of the cellblock is completely empty.

You start walking again, but within a minute, you hear the footsteps again. You whip your head around, but again, no one is there!

"What is that?" Taryn asks, her eyes wide.

Turn the page.

"Come on, we're almost to the front lobby. Let's just keep moving," you tell her.

As you turn back to keep walking, you instantly feel sick to your stomach. Up ahead, where the main entrance to Alcatraz was just visible, is a wall of blue-gray fog. The front desk, lobby, and the cells are all gone.

The wall of fog appears to be moving toward you. You're trapped between the phantom footsteps behind you and the wall of mystery fog in front of you.

To keep going toward the fog, go to page 85.

To run back toward The Hole, turn to page 89.

"It's probably just fog coming in off the water," you tell Taryn. "Someone just left the doors open. Let's go."

Your heart is racing as you head toward the ominous cloud. When you get closer, you hear a strange hissing sound coming from within it.

"Let's just run through it," you tell Taryn, grabbing her arm and taking off before she can object. You enter the fog and keep running, even though you can't see a thing. The hissing is much louder in the fog, but before you know it, you pop out the other side and into the lobby of Alcatraz. You are running so fast you almost smash into Mrs. Woodford, who is standing in the crowded lobby with your class.

"Where have you two been?" she says, her voice rising. "Security is searching the whole island for you!"

Turn the page.

You think for a moment, trying to decide if you should tell Mrs. Woodford the truth. Will she really believe Alcatraz is haunted? If she thinks you're lying, you'll get in even bigger trouble!

You turn back toward the wall of green fog and find yourself staring down the long cellblock. You see an area marked off with yellow caution tape. Behind it an old radiator hisses, shooting out a small trail of steam.

Was that the "fog" you were trapped in? Just then you hear the phantom footsteps, loud and echoing, as they get closer. You look up and see a hulking man in a security uniform. His shiny black dress shoes click hard on the concrete with every step.

"Are these the two we've been searching for?" the man asks.

"Yes," she replies, scowling at you and Taryn. She firmly guides you toward the front doors with the rest of your class watching.

You turn to Taryn, who returns the same confused look. The phantom footsteps, the fog—was your mind playing tricks on you? Did you get so scared you began to imagine things? You turn around to look for the fog, but instead you see the ghost of Robert Stroud.

Robert Stroud was also known as The Birdman of Alcatraz. He spent 30 years at Leavenworth Prison and another 17 at Alcatraz.

Turn the page.

As you lock eyes with the dead man, Stroud raises a bony arm and points right at you. With a wave of his hand, a dozen birds appear overhead, then dive at you. The birds look as dead as their creator, but with beaks and talons you're sure could rip you to pieces. You cover your head, but the birds swarm you. You've fallen victim to The Birdman of Alcatraz.

THE END

To follow another path, turn to page 13.
To learn more about Alcatraz, turn to page 101.

You're not even sure the footsteps were real, but the fog is absolutely real ... and terrifying! You and Taryn turn back and head toward The Hole while staying alert for the sound of footsteps.

On your left you see the entrance to the prison mess hall. Without stopping to think, you burst through the doors in search of an exit.

Inmates received three meals a day, served cafeteria-style in the prison mess hall.

Turn the page.

Instead you find yourself in the lunchroom of Alcatraz sometime in the past. There are more than 100 men in the mess hall in the middle of a riot. A burly inmate throws a folding chair at you, just missing your head. You and Taryn take cover in the corner as convicts throw food trays, garbage cans, and anything else not nailed down.

The food at Alcatraz was considered to be the best prison food. Quality was high and everyone always got enough.

While you try to make sense of what's happening, the riot escalates. The guards have lost control, and the inmates have barricaded the doors to keep the other guards out. They begin setting fire to anything that will burn.

You look for a way out of the mess hall as smoke starts to fill the room. You and Taryn drop to the ground, trying to stay below the smoke and flying objects. The inmates have gone to war, and you're trapped in the crossfire!

The smoke becomes thicker, and your eyes are burning. You soon feel yourself losing consciousness. You gasp for air, taking your final breaths inside a ghastly prison riot at Alcatraz.

THE END

To follow another path, turn to page 13.
To learn more about Alcatraz, turn to page 101.

Taryn pulls you to your feet. You made a terrible mistake leaving your class, but you're going to make sure Taryn gets back safely. You begin to run as fast as you can down a narrow hall leading toward cellblock B. The hall seems miles long, and your legs are burning. You desperately want to stop, but whatever or whoever closed those cell doors is back there.

You run past the cell of Al Capone, past where gangster Mickey Cohen stayed, and where the infamous Anglin brothers bunked. You were excited to see their cells, to see how they tunneled out the back in the only successful escape in the history of Alcatraz. But now, that's the last thing on your mind.

You're running so fast when you turn the next corner that you almost slam head-on into Mrs. Woodford.

Clarence Anglin, Jon Anglin, and Frank Morris, the three
men who attempted escape on June 11, 1962

"Where have you two been?" she asks.
"I've been worried sick!"

"There is a ghost, the cell doors slammed
shut, and there wasn't a single person in the entire
prison!" you stammer, gasping for air.

"If you think you're going to get out of being
punished by making up a story like that, you're
sadly mistaken," she says, frowning.

Turn the page.

"We're not lying," you insist. "Come look, see for yourself!"

You lead Mrs. Woodford back and peer nervously around the corner. You can't believe your eyes. The hall is filled with hundreds of tourists. People are snapping pictures, exploring the cells, and taking in Alcatraz.

More than one million people visit Alcatraz every year to see, among other things, Al Capone's cell.

Where did they all come from? you wonder. You and Taryn exchange a confused look. Is it possible that you imagined the entire thing? It all felt so real.

You drop your head as you and Taryn slink back to your class and start walking toward the main doors. You stop to bend down and tie your shoes, but your eyes widen at the sight of thick green goo on your sneaker.

The footsteps WERE real! You catch up to Taryn and show her your sneaker. The two of you share a look as you step gratefully outside into the bright California sunshine.

THE END

To follow another path, turn to page 13.
To learn more about Alcatraz, turn to page 101.

You both jump to your feet and sprint down the hall toward the main entrance. You've never run this fast in your life, and you don't stop until you hit the front doors and burst outside. You look around for a security guard, a family of tourists—anyone who can help. But the grounds of Alcatraz are eerily quiet. Then you see a man to your left who is feeding a huge flock of birds. A park ranger—you're saved!

You make your way toward the man, who slowly raises his head and watches you and Taryn approach.

"What are you kids doing down here?" the man asks as you walk up.

"We're on a field trip with our class, but we decided to do a little exploring," you tell him, noticing his unusual outfit.

"So no one knows you are out here?" he questions.

It strikes you as an odd question, but you simply say, "No."

"Good," he says, smiling to reveal a mouthful of crooked, rotten teeth. Then you see a string of letters and numbers on his uniform: AZ-594. That prison number belonged to Robert Stroud, The Birdman of Alcatraz!

The man sees the terror in your eyes and smiles. "Do you like birds?" he asks.

"Yyyyeeeessss," you stammer out, hoping that's what he wanted you to say.

"Good," he says with a laugh. "Then you'll love my birds. Dinner time!" Stroud takes the bucket of seed and throws it in the air, raining birdseed down all around you.

Turn the page.

Instantly, the massive flock of birds takes off, then dive bombs straight at you and Taryn. You cover your heads and squat down, hoping to protect yourself from dozens of sharp beaks.

The birds form a tight circle around you and swirl like a tornado, faster and faster until they are a big blur. The ground beneath you begins to spin. Then, as fast as they began their assault, the birds suddenly dart for the sky and are gone.

You flutter your eyes open anxiously and look around. The Birdman is gone too, but somehow, you're not outside anymore. You're in Stroud's cell inside Alcatraz!

You push on the cell door, but it doesn't budge. The cell is empty, just a metal cot, a sink, and a toilet. There's nothing to help you break out. You slump down to the floor and bury your face in your hands.

Why did I decide to leave the class? you think worriedly. Suddenly, a greenish-yellow vapor pours in under the door of the cell.

"What is that?" yells Taryn.

A shape begins to appear within the vapor. Within seconds, the face of The Birdman appears, followed by the rest of his body, floating inches off the floor.

"They never let me have birds here at Alcatraz," Stroud grunts, "But they never said I couldn't keep a couple of kids as pets!"

THE END

To follow another path, turn to page 13.
To learn more about Alcatraz, turn to page 101.

Alcatraz prison closed its doors on March 21, 1963.

EPILOGUE: THE ROCK

Alcatraz Federal Penitentiary locked away its first prisoners on August 11, 1934. The prison was a converted military facility on Alcatraz Island in the middle of San Francisco Bay. Alcatraz was built to house the most dangerous prisoners in the federal prison system. Alcatraz consisted of the main prison, plus more than a half dozen other buildings where prisoners worked and guards and their families lived. Alcatraz housed between 200 and 300 prisoners at any given time. These men were often violent criminals, bank robbers, arsonists, and murderers.

Escaping from Alcatraz was considered impossible. Any man who made it to the water faced strong currents, sharks, and frigid water. He would also have to swim more than a mile to make it to shore.

Despite the long odds, 36 men tried to escape from Alcatraz. Most were captured. Some were shot and killed by the guards. Others drowned trying to swim away.

Alcatraz closed 29 years after the first prisoner walked through its doors, but some people claim that the prison is still inhabited.

The Golden Gate Bridge can be seen from the outer edges of Alcatraz.

Rumors of ghost sightings and unexplained events have swirled around Alcatraz for years. Thanks in part to the tales of ghosts, ghouls, and terror, Alcatraz attracts more than 1.5 million visitors each year.

Dozens of prisoners were shot, stabbed, beaten, and tortured inside the prison walls. Do their spirits remain on the island today? There are plenty of skeptics who believe the stories of the paranormal happenings on Alcatraz Island are just that—stories. Nothing but urban legends and spooky tales. But to those who claim to have had a paranormal experience on the island, the ghosts are very real.

In 2014 a couple on vacation from England stopped in one of the cells to snap a photo out one of the small windows. But what they saw in the photo surprised them.

The Alcatraz Ghost Woman appears to be dressed in clothing from the 1930s or 1940s.

The couple saw a woman staring through the window at the camera. It is evident she isn't another tourist. In fact, the couple says she appeared to be from another time period altogether. They described seeing a dark female figure in the picture. When the tourists looked out the window of the cell, no one was there. They remain convinced they saw a ghost.

James Johnston, the warden from 1934 to 1948, didn't believe in ghosts until giving a tour one day. He heard a woman sobbing, but it wasn't anyone in his group. Instead, the sobbing was coming from behind the walls. The moment the crying stopped, a frigid wind blew through the cellblock.

Guards patrolling Alcatraz Island have also reported ghostly encounters. Some claimed to hear cannons firing, even though cannons hadn't been used on the island since its days as a military prison. Another time, guards reported a ghostly visitor at a Christmas party at the warden's home on the island. The apparition was there, and then instantly gone.

In the end, the debate over whether Alcatraz Island is haunted may never be solved. Skeptics will doubt, believers will believe, and tourists will continue to visit the legendary prison to decide for themselves.

TIMELINE

1775—Spanish explorer Juan Manuel de Ayala first visits the island. He names it "Isla de los Alcatraces," or "Island of the Pelicans."

November 1, 1850—President Millard Fillmore designates Alcatraz for military use.

1853—Construction of a fort begins.

1854—The first lighthouse on the Pacific coast is built on the island.

1861—Alcatraz becomes the official military prison on the Pacific coast.

March 1863—Confederate sympathizers load the *J.M. Chapman* with weapons. They are caught, arrested, and imprisoned at Alcatraz.

1895—A group of 19 Hopi Indians are sent to Alcatraz for not adopting white culture. They are imprisoned for nearly a year.

January 1, 1934—The Federal Bureau of Prisons takes over the island.

August 23, 1934—Al Capone arrives at Alcatraz. He spends more than four years on the island.

1935—Joe Bowers is the first to try to escape. Wounded, he falls down a cliff and is killed.

August 1936—Alvin Karpis is sent to Alcatraz, where he stays until April 1962. He is the island's longest-serving prisoner.

December 1937—Theodore Cole and Ralph Roe are the first to escape the prison. They are never seen again, but are presumed drowned before they reach the mainland.

May 1946—The most serious escape attempt, later called the Battle of Alcatraz, takes place. Two officers and three prisoners are killed, with 17 officers and one prisoner wounded.

June 11, 1962—Frank Morris and Jon and Clarence Anglin escape by digging holes in the concrete around the air vents in their cells. They are never seen again.

March 21, 1963—Alcatraz closes its doors; the last 27 convicts leave the island in leg irons and handcuffs.

1964—Sioux Indians try to claim Alcatraz Island as part of the Treaty of Fort Laramie, which returned out-of-use federal lands to Indians of All Tribes, a group of American Indians.

November 9, 1969—The Indians of All Tribes reclaim the island. It turns into the longest occupation of a federal facility by Native Americans, lasting until June 11, 1971.

1972—Alcatraz becomes part of the Golden Gate National Recreation Area. It opens for public tours the following year.

GLOSSARY

cellblock (SEL-blok)—a section of a prison containing a large number of cells

ectoplasm (EK-toh-PLA-suhm)—a slimy substance associated with ghosts; some people believe ghosts leave ectoplasm behind when they interact with the real world.

eternity (ee-TUR-nuh-tee)—a measure of time that never ends

illuminate (i-LOOM-eh-nayt)—to light up an object or area

instinct (IN-stingkt)—behavior that is natural rather than learned

isolation (eye-suh-LAY-shun)—the condition of being alone

orb (ORB)—a glowing ball of light that sometimes appears in photographs taken at reportedly haunted locations

paranormal (pair-uh-NOR-muhl)—having to do with an unexplained event that has no scientific explanation

penitentiary (pen-uh-TEN-chur-ee)—a prison for people found guilty of serious crimes

riot (RYE-uht)—to act in a violent and often uncontrollable way

ruins (ROO-ins)—the remains of something that has collapsed or been destroyed

skeptic (SKEP-tik)—a person who questions things that other people believe in

smuggle (SMUHG-uhl)—to bring something or someone into or out of a country illegally

solitary confinement (SOL-uh-ter-ee kon-FINE-mehnt)— keeping prisoners isolated and away from other prisoners; sometimes used as a form of punishment or protection.

specter (SPEK-tur)—a ghost

terrain (tuh-RAYN)—the surface of the land

transparent (transs-PAIR-uhnt)—easily seen through

urban legend (UR-behn LEJ-uhnd)—a modern story with little or no evidence that supports the premise; urban legends often have scary plots

vantage point (VAN-tij POINT)—a position that gives you a better view to see something

vapor (VAY-pur)—a gas made from a liquid

warden (WOR-duhn)—the person officially in charge of a prison

OTHER PATHS TO EXPLORE

In this book you've seen how terrifying being alone in a haunted place can be. But haunted places can mean different things to different people. Seeing an experience from many points of view is an important part of understanding it.

Here are a few ideas for other haunted points of view to explore:

+ Although there are no specific "haunted" tours, guides and visitors alike have reported hearing noises, strange sights, and other supernatural events. Imagine you're a ghost hunter exploring the island. What kinds of paranormal gear would you bring? Where would you explore first? What would it be like?

+ Imagine being locked up on Alcatraz. How far would you go to escape? What would your plan be to get off the island?

+ What would it have been like to be a guard at Alcatraz, surrounded by dangerous prisoners? Would you feel powerful, or terrified? Are there any prisoners you would want to avoid?